Liturgy

By A. Malone

Table of Contents:

For Josh

Love you always

Introduction:

Church is a good and wonderful place for many people. For many other people, it is not. As a child growing up with chronic illness, church was a distressing context to learn a myriad of confusing and conflicting facts about life, God, self, and the world.

This little book contains an exploration of that chrysalis as it was for my growing up, the teeth it helped me cut and the claws it helped me sharpen. I hope it will resonate for you who have experienced trauma of the spiritual or physical variety in your youths.

Join the pack. We are stronger together.

Did someone trace you away with her fingertips
Drawing out the open wound inside?
Did someone drop words like stones in a bag
Wrapping the weight tight to your throat?
Did the empty air of no-one wrap your skin all
around
Taking your breath into vacuum
Crumpling your rib cage
A rip in the skin
Healed open
So the wind whistles through?

Have you stuffed your bones with rags of comfort
Flossing them through the holes between
Have you painted your skin red with a knife
And your face black with the char
From the burning
And burning
That screams in your head?

Have you stood at the window
Over the street
Counting the pros and cons
Of falling?

Have they told you it gets better?

Do the platitudes slide from your oil-slick feathers
Dripping to puddle between your toes
Draining way to wherever they store them
Recycle them
Dump them on your head again?

Have they told you it gets better?

Do you know the inspirational posters by heart
now
That tell you about permanent solutions to
temporary problems
To permanent problems a temporary solution
As if they've walked a mile in your shoes
When you never took them off
And handed them over?

Have they told you it gets better?

Have you rehearsed how when Middle School
High School
College
This Job
This Marriage
Is over it will all be better?

It's a well-meant exercise in compassion
Rehearsed before the mirror
Delivered with the right expression
It's ok
They love you
It gets better

But the wind whistles through the holes in your
body for decades
You sit on the burning floor of your burning mind
Skin peeling away and flaking upward as wafting
ash
The voices call-and-responding in a catechism of
misery
All mixed up in a thousand-thousand voices
Crowding standing room only in the whistling
burning echoing not-getting-better

And we know the secret:
It doesn't have to get better

We are an army
We wage war by getting dressed
We go to Target
We paint our hair and our nails and our bedrooms
We date
We write thorny poetry and draw dead things
We get out of bed
We eat
We text back sometimes two days later but we do
it
We put the knife down
We take only one pill as directed by our doctor
We shower
We use a shot glass to measure
We write

Maybe it doesn't get better
Maybe it never gets better
But we are worthy
Better or not

1: All raised…

Words in skin
Like a named child
The tattoo of a heartbeat
    not enough
        not enough
            not enough

The Mothers they tell us
Our lives are shaped by our sins

Why must these bones
Be our doing/undoing?

When you crafted them in mud and saliva
And gifted them all in blood-red bows?

The story they told us:

The shepherd breaks the lamb's leg
Carries her over his shoulders
So, helpless, she can learn his voice
If you would just learn his voice
Little Lamb
He wouldn't have to keep breaking you
Over
And
Over
Again

The fuck kind of shepherd
Does that

Children are to be seen and not heard:

It is not enough
To sit on the sidelines
Please, dear
Do it quietly

My daddy taught me to pray
Walking through the snow on Saturday
To the place where he'd lay his soul bare with his
friends
Unending rocking, singing, hands lifted like the
bare broken trees we saw drifting on our way here
Spilling remixes of rote memorization
Flash cards of faith flipping over the floor like
Texas hold-'em
High pairs bringing comfort
And miracles on royal flushes

My mama taught me to pray
In the dark closet of my brother's room
Hanging up dress shirts the torn curtain to my
holiest of holies
A stuffed panda bear my priest
Shrieks and slaps and slamming cabinet doors the
uninvited choir outside my chapel
Like the woman with the tambourine who's not
on the band but shows up every Sunday and plays
anyway from the aisles
She's off-beat and unwelcome but church
wouldn't be church without her

My body taught me to pray
Knees screaming at me to get on them
Stay on them
Not abandon them
Keep my DNA like a relic on an altar, unuseful
but cherished, pouring out the tinctures, offering
hours, saying my Our Father's
Static in my bones the daily catechism
Self-flagellation of existence

I have always known how to pray
From the bottom of my soul controlled the
narrative
from "Dear God" to "Amen"
Until I didn't
Until I outgrew it
Until I need a new teacher

Teach me to pray like a leaf turns red in
September
Teach me to pray like a hug from a stranger
Teach me to pray like a salmon dying after she
has laid down her babies
Teach me to pray like the ash off a cigarette
Teach me to pray like a kid not ready for bed yet
Teach me to pray in melody and harmony both
Teach me to pray choked on emotion
Teach me to fucking pray some true shit for once
in my goddamn life

And let all the people I have ever been say

Amen

A confession to the Mothers:

I
Will never need you
Hope makes the heart sick
After all

You were a beach
And I
Racing through the surf
Looking for your happiness
Like sea-glass
Rare and shining
Pausing for a moment on the shore
For my little fingers to snatch at
Before the waves crashed in again
And they were gone

I have never wanted to believe
That everything bad that happens is my fault

You were a riptide
And I
Wading in heedless
Half-drowning to be near you
The bits of sea-glass all collected
Sand-crusted in my yellow bucket
As my sacred offering of child-love
To a towering wave

I have never wanted to believe
That every pain I feel is my own fault

You were a shoreline
And I
Running over your stones
Absorbing your salt
'Til it dried out my skin
Taking in your sea-salt spray
To every single pore of me
Just so when you calmed I would be there
To hear the lapping waves hiss
I love you

I have never wanted to believe
That every drop I bleed is my own fault

I can't survive all this believing

2: …To Be Good Girls…

Hold our souls
Up to the light
And tell me
About all the places
They match

Catechism

Question 1: What is to be done with dragons?
Answer 1: Good girls kill their dragons
Bravely slay the monsters
Hidden in their chests

Dogs of the desert
We laugh through broken teeth
Dance on bloodied feet
Horrify them
Until they shout
"Bow your heads
Suffer in sober-minded self-reflection
How can you learn the lessons of pain
If you just
Keep
Laughing"
We hear and click our forked tongues
Knowing if we comply
we die
While living

Are our groanings and gnashings holy enough for
you?

Catechism

Question 2: What is to be done with beasts?
Answer 2: Good girls never feed the beasts
Under their beds at night
Or behind their closet doors

At last to be
A victor
Rather than
A warrior
Warpaint melted to makeup
Swords to plow shares
War stories by hearths
Of battles long ago

Catechism

Question 3: What is to be done with teeth?
Answer 3: File them down

We have spent
too many years
Watching the shadows
Shift in one house/room/couch/pillow
To be less than ravenous
Now

Catechism

Question 4: What is to be done with teeth?
Answer 4: ~~File them down~~
Good girls rarely survive Armageddon
They can't fend off the horsemen
Without teeth and fang and fire-breath
From the monsters and dragons
They were taught to kill

If the way we tear into
   life's
      red
         flesh
Frightens/disgusts/horrifies you

   Look away

    Look away

To think
After all this time
We should find one another
Healed
Yet with the same scars

Don't leave yourself alone so much
Who knows what you'll do
Without you

3: … Just Like Me

Though beaten
    battered
        even buried it may be
My soul is a diamond
    brilliant
        unbreakable
And at the end of the bitterest road
    will march on
        blinding

        and unscathed

And what is a soul
Without an altar
On which to give up
All it has?

Here in the tangle of carpet and sunlight
Here where the curtains drift soft in the breeze
Up where the ceiling fan ruffles your arm hair
And the soft-drifting sun motes compel you to
sneeze

Deep in the wilds of tubes and of needles
Wrapped in a mess of yesterday's clothes
Look up for a moment and take a deep breath, love
There are thousands of us, you are never alone

We are the Lost Ones
Fallen from life
Fighting a lost war
With a dull knife
Welcome to the Lost Ones
Come meet your new King
Listen, I'll teach you incredible things
Go pick up your needles, your bottles, your sticks
I'll show you how capable, how mighty the Sick

Getting the drop on the wisdom of ages
Skipping ahead to the end of the tale
We follow no leaders, no hiding, no seeking
We grow up out of order here, aged and hale

In our world we each of us sport our own hook
A badge of our bravery in battle's fresh heat
We sleep with the wolves, walk gently with bears
And tick-tocking alligators sleep at our feet

We are the Lost Ones
Floating below
With blood on our faces
And scars in our bones
Welcome to the Lost Ones
Come be our new King
I'll listen, you teach me incredible things
Go pick up your needles, your bottles, your sticks
We know just how capable, how mighty the Sick

We don't want to be here
Don't want to stay more
But giving up's not an option
In Always Evermore

I am a scavenger
Picking life from the bones of living
Waiting in the wings for precious dregs
All but drained away
I listen to this dinner eaten for survival
Fill me halfway
Anticipating the ache of rising from this hunt
Feet bloodied with the chase
After leftover feasts

And my heart tells me
Even here, love, there is living

There are no tomorrows
Just today
    today

        today

I was sanctified once
And everything
Everything mattered
The sun rose in my mouth
Every time I spoke

But I have sat with myself
Until I know her
Nothing can surprise me now

I took my confession
And time
Time ticked quicker
The hellhounds nipped at my heels
Every time I slowed down

But I have listened to my breath
Until it gave up its secrets
Nothing can rush me now

(Read this one out loud)

It gets dark in the beginning
A long dark start to the heart of the grocery cart
you throw everything in
Until it wears thin
Until you go in
All in
Sin

Just a little at first then you're in the middle of the
mess of the confession that
You like this
And it won't even start to get past the part of your
lips because you can't admit it
Even to yourself
The pain is safety
it's home
it's all that you know it's so familiar unshown to
anyone how
alone feels less than lonely when it's just me in
the middle of the can-despite-all-this that makes
me feel helpless yet powerful
I am powerful

Full of the ability to overcome
(Didn't you say I was an overcomer?)
And deep in the recesses of my lungs unable to
make the trek to my tongue is the truth my heart
leaves continually unsung the truth that I can't get
any more
That this is all I have to live for
That I'm sure the lure of the healthy could get me
but I can't get it
So I rest it
On the carpet
Of the kneeler
Where my knees are
Swollen
Hold on
I may be broken but I've done more with s o r e
sore than you've ever done with s o a r soar

So what's your success in the half-grown press of
your hourly middle-management laundry on the
weekends wife life
Because mine is glorious
Mine is fucking victorious
I win

Acknowledgements:

My husband, Colin, for giving me forever.

My Okadas, for being my safe home then, now, and always.

My first therapist, Nora, for showing me the way.

My dear friends and test readers: Gabe, Aidan, Liane, Charis, and Jeff.

My dear friend and cover designer Katie Martin for volunteering her time out of pure love.

Made in the USA
Middletown, DE
02 April 2021